# A
# RIDE
# TO
# ETERNITY

---

## FROM ITALY TO AMERICA:

### THE TRAGIC STORY OF A
### YOUNG WOMAN'S MURDER

---

BOB IANARELLI

Print ISBN: 978-1-0983-4147-3

eBook ISBN: 97-81-09834-148-0

To Steve Antony:

Not quite the book that we often threatened to write together, but it's the best that I could muster alone. Miss you my friend.

# CONTENTS

# MAPS

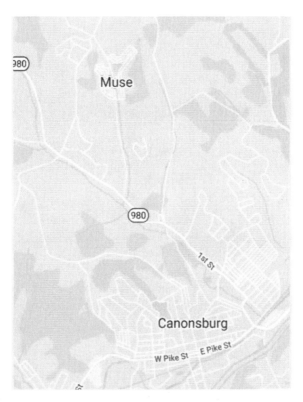

**Maps courtesy of Google Maps**

# PROLOGUE

SHE was left for dead along a lonely country lane on a warm fall afternoon in 1939. Her comatose body was discovered with a badly fractured skull lying beneath the wheels of a parked car along a seldom travelled road between Canonsburg and Muse, Pennsylvania. Maria Luisa (Mary) Iannarelli (pronounced Eye-na-relli), a beautiful, vibrant, teenage girl just blossoming into womanhood had been mortally injured and was lying in the dirt in the waning afternoon sun. After hours of struggling to stay alive, she finally passed away the next day at Canonsburg General Hospital.

How she arrived at such a premature end is a question that is shrouded in as much mystery today as it was at the time of the incident. The details that emerged after the completion of the investigations were provided solely by the perpetrator of the crime. How much of his version was actually true and how much was provided to the authorities in order to minimize the potential penalty for his actions was a question that haunted her family until their own passing many years later. Considering that a death had occurred under highly unusual circumstances, the final sentence handed down by the court seemed insignificant for the magnitude of the crime. However, the scales of justice sometimes have a habit of meting out punishment in their own way when human endeavors fail.

The events related herein took place in Washington County in the southwestern corner of Pennsylvania. Canonsburg and Muse are located about three miles apart and both are approximately twenty miles southwest of Pittsburgh, Pennsylvania. Most of the residents are honest, hard-working, and blue-collar people. Since the late nineteenth century, coal mining and heavy manufacturing dominated the economies of the towns. The available work was a magnet for anyone seeking a job, including the many immigrants living in the United States. The borough of Canonsburg was founded by John Canon and incorporated in 1802. Although not a large community, it is by far the larger of the two towns where this story takes place.

In the 1800's, Canonsburg's claim to fame was that it was home to Jefferson College, which professed to be the first college west of the Allegheny Mountains. Following the Civil War, both Jefferson College and Washington College in nearby Washington, Pennsylvania were short of funds and students. In order to consolidate the expenses as well as the available students, a merger to form present-day Washington & Jefferson College in Washington took place in 1865. Although a blow to the Canonsburg economy, Canonsburg went on to establish several large manufacturing operations in the borough. These operations kept the economy vibrant and the population fairly steady at around ten thousand people well into the twentieth and twenty first centuries. Over the years, Canonsburg has produced numerous world-class athletes, as well as several noted singers and entertainers, including Perry Como and Bobby Vinton.

Muse was founded in 1922 when the H.C. Frick Coke Company decided to open a coal mine there. The town was named for Charles A. Muse, the Superintendent of Coal Shipments for the company. H.C. Frick was a subsidiary of

National Mining Company, which in turn was a subsidiary of the U.S. Steel Corporation. The land on which Muse was laid out was previously farmed by three unrelated families. In all likelihood, the area would have remained as farmland had H.C. Frick not come along and purchased the land to build the mine and the community. The mine that Frick opened in Muse became known as National #3, but to the locals, it was always the Muse Mine. The mine operated until 1954, when it was finally shut down, putting five hundred men out of work. Although Mary's death took place between Canonsburg and Muse in 1939, her story began an ocean away and eighteen years earlier.

Mary - 1939

# CHAPTER 1

## ITALY

—

Mary was born on January 1, 1921, in Barisciano (Bar-ee-sha-no), Italy. When she arrived, she was a true New Year's blessing for her parents, Carlantonio (Carlo) Iannarelli and Irena (Irene) D'Alessandro Iannarelli. She was the second of two children resulting from the marriage. Her older brother, Robert, had been born a little less than two years earlier. Both the Iannarelli and D'Alessandro families resided in Barisciano for as long as anyone could remember. Both names appear in town records as far back as the seventeenth century. They were surrounded by many friends and relatives who helped the young family in a manner common for the Italian culture of the time. It was expected that the family would remain in Barisciano as their forebears had done for centuries. That would have been the case until the economics of post-World War I Italy intervened.

Barisciano is a small village in the Abruzzo region of Italy. It lies at the foothills of the Eastern slope of the Apennine Mountains in Central Italy. The nearest city of any real size is L'Aquila, about fifteen miles to the north. Barisciano is approximately seventy miles due east of Rome, and about fifty miles to the west of the Adriatic Sea. Other than a common language, there is not much else in Barisciano that could be confused with

Rome's Italy. Narrow cobblestone streets, barely wide enough for one car to pass, wind their way through the village. The homes are mostly attached two-story stucco affairs. With the exception of their very old age, they are reminiscent of row homes that are found in many American cities. Most of the homes have small vegetable gardens to the rear, saving the occupants trips to the market in the spring and summer months. Except for the automobiles and electric lights found today, one could easily conclude that time has stood still in Barisciano. In the 1920's, as you will also find today, the narrow streets, the church, and the stucco homes dominated the architecture of the hamlet.

**Street in Barisciano**

The main Roman Catholic Church is centrally located in the village. The primary church is one of the dominant buildings, and it always was and continues to be the force that dictates the rhythm and flow of life, both culturally and socially in the town. Like the rest of Italy, most holidays are church-related celebrations, such as the Feast of the Assumption that takes place in

August. Businesses close and a large parade takes place, with the statue of the Virgin leading the way. Children's progress towards adulthood is measured by church-mandated milestones such as the First Communion and Confirmation. Because the seat of the Catholic Church is located in Rome, all of Italy has been governed by the church doctrine and discipline for many centuries.

Roman Catholic Church - Barisciano

Schooling for children born in the town during the 1920's could be described as erratic at best. Most children went to school for four or five years and the girls usually attended for a shorter time than the boys. As they grew older, the boys were often sent to learn a trade by working as apprentices. Common trades at the time were tailoring, carpentry, shoemaking, black-smithing, stone masonry, and other practical vocations needed to keep the progress of the village flowing. Girls left school by the age of nine or ten. They stayed at home helping their mothers with household chores until marriage took them away. It was into this town and culture that Mary was born in 1921.

Mary's parents, Carlo and Irene, were both born in Barisciano in the 1890s. Carlo was born in 1894, the son of Francesco Iannarelli and Frances Veglia. His paternal grandmother bore the name Maria Luisa (Marinelli) and the name subsequently got passed on to his only daughter. Carlo was the youngest of three sons. His eldest brother, Oreste, was born in 1890 and died after just three months of life. His other brother, Eduardo, was born in 1892. He also died in infancy after surviving for seven months. Life expectancy was short and infant deaths were common at that time in Italy as well as in the rest of the world. Though Carlo was the youngest of three sons, he came into the world an only child and remained so for the rest of his life.

While Carlo was still a young boy, his father left for Brazil. It was not unusual in those days for Italians to emigrate to any of a number of South American countries. High immigration quotas and relative ease in entering the countries often made these the preferred alternatives to the United States. Francesco was seeking better employment and a better way of life for his family. Jobs and economic opportunities were few in Barisciano as was true of all of Italy. This fact more than any other fueled the mass migration to the Americas in the late nineteenth and early part of the twentieth centuries. Francesco planned to travel to Brazil and find work. When he had accumulated enough money, he would then send for his wife and son. In the meantime, he would send what he could on a regular basis in order to support his family back in Italy. However, after sending one check and two letters, he was never heard from again. Whether he met an untimely death, met another woman and married again, or disappeared for another unknown reason is a mystery. His small family was left without any visible means of support.

Little did Carlo know at the time that he would follow a similar path later in his life but with very different results.

After several years of school, Carlo's formal education ended when he became an apprentice in the shoemaking and repair trade. His mother took to sewing and doing laundry to provide some income for herself and her son. With her meager earnings, help from close family, and Carlo's earnings as an apprentice shoemaker, the small family struggled to survive for several years. Although difficult, the situation was relatively stable until 1914 when World War I began.

Italy was originally allied with Germany before the war started, but declared itself neutral when the fighting began. Italy had only become a sovereign nation a little more than fifty years earlier and was not as industrialized as other nations of the time. Therefore, it was not in a strong position to fight a protracted war. Nevertheless, when the signatory Allies to the Treaty of London promised Italy eventual control of disputed lands along the six hundred-mile border with Austria if they entered the war, Italy declared war on its northern neighbor, Austria-Hungary on May 23, 1915. The caveat to securing the disputed land was that the war ended with an Allied victory.

Initially, Italy managed to mobilize 1.2 million men, including Carlo Iannarelli, who had been drafted into the service of his country. They were primarily sent to attack the Austrians in Tyrol. By the time the war ended, the number of Italians under arms had swelled to five million men. The fighting was mostly in mountainous territory with bitter cold winter weather. Nearly as many men perished from avalanches and frostbite as from enemy actions. Neither side made much progress, but the carnage on both sides was incomprehensible. The stalemate continued until October, 1917 when Germany joined the fray to help Austria. This led to the Battle of Caporetto, where the Germans and Austrians finally won a convincing victory. This victory was soon offset by aid to Italy from Britain and the United States, which simply perpetuated the bloody stalemate. By the time the fighting stopped in November, 1918, Italy had lost over 600,000 troops and another 900,000 were disabled by some kind of injury. Most of these troops were either killed in action, died from untreated wounds suffered in battle, or were affected in some way from exposure to the cold. The fighting was a bloodbath of poison gas, artillery, mortar fire, and machine guns. Even more disturbing was how Italy's own military police participated by forcing the soldiers forward into enemy fire with guns at their backs. All this sacrifice was done in order to acquire a strip of almost worthless land along a disputed border. In the end, it all proved to be for naught. Although Italy annexed some token conquered territory in South Tyrol and the city of Bolzano, she never did receive all the regional land as promised after the Allied victory by the Treaty of London,.

Although severely wounded, Carlo suffered a better fate than most of the Italian troops. He also fared better than his country. During one of the battles in 1917, a mortar shell landed near Carlo and other men in his immediate unit. When the shell exploded, a large fragment hit Carlo in the side and rendered him unconscious. When he woke up he found himself in a field hospital, severely wounded and in a serious condition. He was eventually moved to a hospital in northern Italy where he began the long, slow road to recovery. By the time he had sufficiently healed from his wounds, the war was nearing an end. He was soon discharged and sent back to Barisciano. Carlo had always been reluctant to discuss his wartime exploits. His wounds were as much mental as they were physical. The scar on his side was evidence of the great trauma that he had endured.

Two aspects of his wartime experience haunted him. He frequently questioned why, out of all the men with whom he had entered the service, to his knowledge he was the only one who had survived. He often felt guilty for being the only one to be spared from the carnage. He also often dwelled on his occasional selection by officers' orders to participate in a firing squad, which were commonly used as a means to summarily execute deserters in the Italian Army. In order to lessen the mental anguish of having to shoot a fellow soldier, one member of the squad was always given a blank bullet and allegedly nobody knew which person had the blank. Each soldier could therefore rationalize that he had fired the blank and didn't kill his comrade. This was an interesting theory, but Carlo related that the men always knew from the recoil of the rifle if they actually were the ones to fire the blank. He never had the blank.

Upon his return to Barisciano, Carlo renewed his acquaintance with Irene D'Alessandro, a woman with whom he had a budding relationship prior to the war. Irene, like Carlo, was a native of Barisciano and was born there in January, 1898. Her parents, Beatrice and Felix, also had a son, Flaviano, who eventually immigrated to the United States and became a resident of Muse, Pennsylvania. Carlo and Irene were both in their twenties and anxious to get on with their lives after the trauma of the war. They soon married and had a son, Robert, in 1919. One and a half years later, their daughter Mary was born on January 1, 1921. It was a wonderful way to bring in the New Year.

# CHAPTER 2

## COMING TO AMERICA

—

Good economic times did not return to Italy after the war. Although trained in shoemaking, Carlo and his family struggled to keep their heads above water in the years following the cessation of hostilities. Many of their friends and relatives were giving up on Italy and moving to the United States or other countries in Europe and the Americas. By 1921, the situation had deteriorated to the point that leaving seemed like the only sensible alternative. These thoughts were reinforced by letters from friends and family who had gone to America and quickly found jobs. The problem was, as it was for many families, there just wasn't enough money for the entire family to go to the United States together. Carlo and Irene made the difficult decision for Carlo to go to America alone, send money back home after he found employment, and eventually save enough to bring the rest of the family to the United States. In retrospect, had they known how many years would pass before the latter came to fruition, they may not have made the decision to separate. Another issue that weighed heavily on their minds, especially Irene's, was the story of Carlo's father leaving and never being heard from again. Was it possible that the same thing could happen to her and her children?

Carlo's Passport Photo - 1921

Despite these misgivings, Carlo left for the United States shortly after Mary's birth in 1921. He had no knowledge of the English language and very little money to help keep him in food and shelter. Prior to leaving Italy, he heard from friends who had already emigrated that there was work for immigrant laborers in Buffalo, New York. After arriving at Ellis Island, Carlo found his way to Buffalo. As promised by his friends, he was able to find work on a construction crew. The project ended after two years, and Carlo was looking for work again. During his time in Buffalo, he had remained in contact with relatives who lived in Detroit, Michigan. Seeing no more opportunity in Buffalo, he moved on to Detroit. Although work was sometime sporadic, he was usually able to remain employed. Between his living expenses and what money he was able to send home to Italy, little was being saved for the family's eventual trip to the

United States. Upon recommendations from other relatives, he moved on to what were perceived as greener pastures, this time in Bellaire, Ohio.

Bellaire, Ohio, lies along the Ohio River across from Wheeling, West Virginia. Coal mining had been sustaining the region for many years. The coal mines were looking for workers, and so Carlo seized the opportunity. Conditions for workers in coal mines in the 1920-s were atrocious; hazards such as dust, floods, cave-ins, and explosions, and low pay, were just some of the dangers that the miners endured. The miners were not paid by the hour. They were paid only for the coal loaded less expenses such as blasting powder and tools. On a bad day it was possible to earn no money at all. After dealing with all the poor conditions, the ultimate insult came on payday when the miners were paid in company script, which could only be spent at the company store. The only way to generate real cash was to sell the script at a discount to anyone willing to buy it. That person would still be required to spend the script at the company store.

Miners everywhere began striking for better working conditions and pay. The mines around Bellaire, Ohio were no different. There were several strikes intermingled with occasional layoffs, which meant that Carlo wasn't making much progress toward bringing his family to America. Fortunately, he had remained in contact with his brother-in-law, Flaviano D'Alessandro, who had also immigrated to America. Flaviano landed in a small town called Muse, Pennsylvania. His wife, Concetta DiNardo, had many relatives in the area, so it was only natural that they would move to Muse to work and live. Flaviano convinced Carlo that the conditions and pay at the coal mine in Muse were much more attractive than those in Bellaire, Ohio. So, in 1929, and for the third time since arriving in the United

States, Carlo moved. As it turned out, Flaviano was right; not only was work available, but it was much more stable. There was also a large Italian-American presence in the community, and close family lived nearby. Carlo was finally able to start saving money after settling in Muse.

In anticipation of the opening of their coal mine in Muse, the H. C. Frick Coke Company began building homes in 1921 to be rented to the miners and their families. The homes were owned and maintained by the company with a full-time crew of carpenters and painters. Over the course of the next five years, over three hundred homes were built to form the small community of Muse, Pennsylvania. The homes were all two story duplexes shared by two families. One family lived on each side. The first floor consisted of two rooms: a kitchen/dining room combination and a living room. The second floor consisted of two bedrooms. All of the houses had a front and back porch as well as a basement. When the homes were first built, there was no indoor plumbing, and so an outhouse was placed in the backyard. Plumbing wasn't added in most homes until many years later. Alongside the outhouse was a coal storage shed, as most homes in Western Pennsylvania were heated by coal at that time.

When Carlo arrived in Muse, he was quickly able to secure a job at National #3 and rent a room from friends who had space for a boarder. The large number of immigrant Italians who had come to Muse at the time gave them all a sense of camaraderie and belonging. Carlo finally began to feel that he had found his niche in the United States.

It was about this time that the origins of the Muse Italian Club (also referred to as the Muse Independent Club) began to take shape. The Italians spent a lot of their spare time socializing in their homes. The number of people able to participate and the types of social activities were always limited by the available space in the homes. In order to overcome this problem, a group of Italian men came together and rented the first floor of a building in the village along the Muse-Bishop Road just past Walnut Street. Larger groups were then able to gather, and the original Italian Club began to take shape. The group soon became so large that they made the decision to formally charter their club and construct their own building.

They secured a parcel of land further along the other side of the Muse-Bishop Road toward the hamlet of Bishop. After several tries they were granted a loan to erect the building to house the club. For its time and location the building was somewhat of an aberration. It was a large, modern, two-story, all-brick building that was quite different from the proliferation of duplex company houses. The first floor consisted of a bar, a dining area, and a Morra* room.

The second floor of the building consisted of a small apartment for the full-time bartender and a ballroom with another bar. The ballroom was used for weddings, New Year's Eve parties, birthday parties, or any other gathering where a large group, including wives and children, could gather. The list of charter members of the club echoes with names from Central and Southern Italy such as Iannarelli, Leonardi, Battistone, Baldini, DiNardo, D'Alessandro, and Batista. The cornerstone of the building was laid in 1937, and the club continues to exist to this day.

> (*Note: Morra is an Italian counting game played by attempting to guess the total number of fingers put out by two opposing players. As a player throws out his fingers he shouts the number in Italian that he thinks the total will be. The player who guesses correctly scores a point and the game continues.)

Cornerstone – Muse Independent Club

Muse Independent Club Today

It was into this comfortable environment that Carlo wished to bring his family. Although the financial picture continued to brighten, government bureaucracy began to interfere with the planning. By the1930-s, the US Government was controlling immigration by limiting the number of travel visas that were issued each year. Predictably, demand was far greater than the supply. It took the Iannarelli family until 1936 to secure the necessary visas and passage to the United States.

Irene Circa 1932

Mary circa 1932

During the period from 1921 through 1936, while Carlo was attempting to gain a foothold in the United States, life in Barisciano was difficult for the small family. Irene was left as a single parent to raise two infants well into their teenage years. Fortunately, her parents were still alive and able to provide living quarters. They along with other relatives assisted the family in whichever way they could. The money that Carlo was able to send covered the bare necessities of their day-to-day needs. When they were old enough, both Robert and Mary attended the village school. After about five years, Robert dropped out of school and became an apprentice tailor. By the time 1936 arrived, Mary had also finished school several years earlier as was the norm for girls in Italy in those days. She helped her mother with household chores, but also continued to read and study whatever she could find. She also often wrote to her father in America, of whom she had no recollection, and expressed her desire to join him there. All that she knew of her father were from a few pictures she had, and the stories that her mother and other family members told her. It was natural that since Irene raised her children alone, she would grow extremely close to both of them during this time.

Irene and Mary circa 1934

Irene, Robert and Mary finally arrived at Ellis Island on September 14, 1936. All immigrants relocating to the United States were routinely given a medical examination upon disembarkation. It was during this exam that doctors found that Robert had an eye infection. As a result of the infection the doctors denied him entry to the country. He was sent back to Italy where his eye problem was quickly remedied. However, he had to wait until early 1937 to secure another visa and travel again to the United States.

Robert Passport Photo 1937

He was finally granted entry on his second attempt. Robert quickly joined the rest of the family in Muse where the newcomers were all assimilating to their new environment. Carlo became acquainted with his daughter who had been an infant when he left, and became reacquainted with his son who had scant memories of him. The family moved into a duplex home on Locust Street in Muse, and at long last began their journey as a united family.

Ianarelli Home in Muse as it Appears Today

# CHAPTER 3

## DEATH AND BURIAL

—

BY all accounts Robert and Mary became well acclimated to their new country. Robert attended school for one year. Since he was nineteen by then, he left school and went to work at the Muse Mine with his father. Mary fit in well in her new home and was an outstanding student. According to reports in the now defunct *Daily Notes* (the Canonsburg newspaper at the time):

### TERMED BRILLIANT PUPIL

*Mary advanced from third grade to eighth grade in one year at the Muse school.(1)*

*A consistent honor student and termed by one of her teachers as "an outstanding and brilliant pupil" Mary Iannarelli\* came to America on September 14, 1936....*

*Unable to speak English, she entered the Muse grade school a week after her arrival in this country and quickly mastered the language to the extent that within a few months she spoke without a trace of an accent. (2)*

*... was a junior this year in the Cecil township high school. She was the winner of the American Legion Auxiliary award in 1937 for being the outstanding girl in the eighth grade class in Cecil Township School. Last year she led the sophomore class in high school.(3)*

Mary was a devout Roman Catholic and when not in school helped her mother with household chores.

*Mary had no enemies and was well known to everybody in the Muse and Cecil districts. Whenever possible she attended the Sunday service at Muse conducted by Rev. Father John Kopera, pastor of the St. Mary's Roman Catholic Church at Cecil, and seldom missed Mass.(4)*

*Mary had no "boy friend" according to her father, and while at home, which was practically all the time while not at school, she helped her mother a great deal and spent long hours studying, which resulted in her high scholastic standing and ability to master English.(5)*

*(\*Note: Throughout the Daily Notes reporting of the incident, they sometimes spelled Mary's last name as Iannarelli and sometimes as Ianarelli. The correct spelling of her version of the name is Iannarelli.)*

By September 1939, the family had settled into a routine and was finally familiar enough with each other that life had become comfortable. Everything suddenly changed on September 23. The day was a sunny and warm fall Saturday. The morning was uneventful and after lunch Mary decided to go to Canonsburg to do some shopping for materials for a sewing project. When she left home it was the last time her family would see her conscious and less than twenty four hours before she was dead.

Although there was regular bus service to and from Canonsburg, Mary chose to take a ride that was offered by a family friend, Frank DiPaola. Mr. DiPaola dropped her in Canonsburg to do her shopping. When finished, she walked to the home of Colombo Pacifico and his wife, Antoinette, her godparents, who resided in the east end of Canonsburg on the corner of Second Street and Moore Avenue.

**The Pacifico House as it Appears Today**

The *Daily Notes* recorded her known travels as follows:

*Checking up on the movement of the girl from the time she left home early in the afternoon, it was determined by this newspaper that she came to Canonsburg on the delivery truck of Frank DiPaola of 600 Highland Ave, East End, who conducts a store at that place.*

*She came to Canonsburg where she made certain purchases and on her way back home she stopped in East Canonsburg at the home of Colombo Pacifico where she spent some time..............(6)*

*......after completing her shopping, she left their home at about 4 PM.*

*Pacifico offered to give her money for bus fare for the trip to Muse, but she declined saying: "I have a lot of work to do and will start walking now. I don't want to ride in the bus on such a nice day as this. I like to get out and walk. (7)*

It was at this point that the mystery begins. The Pacificos were the last people to see her alive and uninjured (except for the perpetrator) before a Mr. Thomas McConnell found her unconscious under his car on Hickman Schoolhouse Road.*

Mary's body was discovered several miles from the Pacifico home. McConnell stated that he found the unconscious body around 4:15 or 4:20. The distance of over two miles from the Pacifico home, and the location where she was found, indicate that it would be impossible for someone to have walked that distance in such a short period of time.

**Location on Angerer (Hickman Schoolhouse) Road**
**Where Mary's Body Was Found.**

*(\*Note: Sometime after 1939 the name of Hickman Schoolhouse Rd. was changed to Angerer Road. Likewise, the name of Engle Road was changed to Burnside Road. The roads were named for the families who happened to be farming the land along the roads at the time. Engle [Burnside] Road begins where it meets Rte.980 [Sometimes referred to as First Street] near the current location of the Turtle Twist Ice Cream Shop. Valley Road, where the perpetrator claimed he was driving that day, ends directly across Rte. 980 from where Burnside Road begins. The most direct route to Muse*

*from Canonsburg is to follow Rte. 980 past Burnside Road and*
*then turn right onto the Muse/Bishop Road. See maps.)*

The *Daily Notes* was not published on weekends. It wasn't until Monday that the events of Saturday, September 23, 1939 were reported. The death of Mary Iannarelli was the headline story and continued to remain so well into the following week.

### Girl Carried to Isolated Spot by Hit & Run Driver
### Left Unconscious Beneath Parked Car Along Highway

*Mary Ianarelli, 18, Muse High School Junior Dies at Canonsburg Hospital 12 Hours Later — Police Search for Man Who Picked Up Body After Striking Girl and Transported It to Lonely Place and Left Her to Die — Found Under Car of Thomas McConnell of Canonsburg*

*State motor police and county authorities today started a search for an automobile driver who is believed to have struck and fatally injured a young girl, then carried her body several miles to an isolated spot on a back road, placed it carefully under the wheels of another car, presumably to lead to the belief that the car under which she was found had struck her.*

*The girl, Mary Ianarelli, 18, of Muse, near here, an American Legion scholarship winner in Cecil Township schools, died at the Canonsburg General hospital some hours after she was found unconscious. She had failed to regain consciousness at any time and thus the mystery of her injury and subsequent death could not be selved (sic) by her own statement.*

*Coroner James B. Jones stated this morning that county and state officers have been working on the case since late Saturday afternoon, when the body of the girl was found and, **although the road between the spot where she was last seen and where she***

28

*was found, has been gone over foot by foot, no trace of an accident
could be found. (Author's emphasis)*

*The girl's body was found under the car of Thomas McConnell, 12
Meadow Lane, Canonsburg, who has a small garden patch in
Cecil Township and who had driven there early Saturday
afternoon to work in the garden. He found the girl under his car
shortly after 4 o'clock and notified authorities without moving
her. When state motor police arrived the girl was extricated and
taken to the hospital unconscious and she died later. A purse and
some dress goods which she had purchased in Canonsburg were
lying at her side. It was declared that the motor of the McConnell
car was cold when officers arrived, indicating the likelihood that it
had not been operated for hours. Investigation showed that the
girl had left East Canonsburg to walk home, about 4 o'clock, thus
exonerating McConnell.*

*According to Mr. McConnell he went to his garden around one
o'clock. The garden is situated in Cecil Township about a mile
and a half from the main highway, along the Hickman school
road. It is approached by a right turn from the highway near the
"Springer" mine.*

*Cpl. George H. Benson took charge of the case with Private J.R.
Fair and W.H. McNary was called for an ambulance. He arrived
with the ambulance and it was necessary to jack up the car
slightly to pull the girl out. She was taken to the Canonsburg
General Hospital, where she died. While in the hospital, she was
unconscious practically all the time. (8)*

The newspaper did not report the type or severity of Mary's
injuries. According to her parents, family, and friends who were
present, the only injury she suffered was severe trauma to the
left side of her head. Her doctors told the family that the wound
could have been made from a narrow pipe, a piece of steel, or
any number of hard, narrow objects. There were no scratches

or scrapes anywhere else on her body, and her clothes were clean and unmarked.

The story continued to dominate the Tuesday, September 26, 1939, issue of the *Daily Notes*. Much of what was published was a reiteration of the previous day's edition. However, the coroner made some discouraging comments that morning.

> *Pennsylvania Motor Police and the county detectives are working on the cahe (sic). Coroner James B. Jones, active in the search for the driver, stated this morning that little, if anything is known of what happened to the girl and was pessimistic as to the likelihood of developing any tangible clue unless something new is uncovered.(9)*

While Carlo and Irene prepared to bury their daughter, the police investigation continued. Her funeral and background story dominated the *Daily Notes* on September 27, 1939. That edition was the longest and most detailed of any reports of the incident.

### Hit-Run Victim Buried Today;
### Many Mourn Mary Iannarelli, of Muse,
### Came to This Country Only Few Years Ago

> *Mary Iannarelli, the 18 year old Muse girl who was killed by a hit-and-run driver, was buried today while hundreds of friends and relatives alternately mourned her death and threated vengeance on her murderer.*
>
> *Brunette, slim and darkly handsome, Miss Iannarelli, a Sophomore in the Cecil township high school and recipient of the American Legion Auxiliary Scholarship medal in 1937 died Sunday morning in the Canonsburg General hospital....*

*While hundreds of schoolmates and friends of the popular girl viewed the body during the past two days in the modest Ianarelli home in Muse, State Motor Police and county authorities were following every clue in an attempt to bring the murderer to justice, but up to this afternoon had made no arrests, and as far as is known, little progress....*

*Carlo Iannarelli, the father, came to America in 1921, "because of the better opportunity" and worked in Bellaire, Ohio, for several years before coming to Muse in 1929.*

*While his wife was prostrate with grief over the death of the only daughter, the father, a giant in stature who is bearing up remarkably under the strain and who has every confidence in the police to bring the murderer to justice, could find no words to express his feeling.*

*"I don't know what to think about it," he replied when asked what he thought about the case. "I think one thing and then get on anoher (sic) 'road' until all is confused."*

*An under-current of resentment against the "killer" has gripped the little mining community, which may flare forth if he is arrested. Chief topic of conversation is the accident and at work, at home and on the streets where little groups of persons gather, the case is discussed from all angles. It is probably the most heart-rending event in the history of the mining community.*

*The Iannarelli family lived happily and comfortably and had planned to have a group photograph taken next Saturday.*

*"Just a few days ago we were talking about having a picture of the four of us taken," the father said. "Since I have been working night turn and Mary has been in school, I never had a chance to see her only on Saturday and Sunday. This Saturday is my day off and we were going to have a photograph taken then. But it is too late now."*

"Mary loved the United States and the freedom of this country," her father said, "and frequently said that she would never go back to Italy even if I tried to force her to do so."

Mary advanced from third to eighth grade in one year at the Muse school. Her father has been an American citizen since 1937 and her brother, Robert, is popular in the community and is recognized as a fine amateur singer. She had completed elementary school in Italy before coming here.

The victim's father emphasized that she frequently said that she would never accept a ride from a stranger which, to some extent discounts the theory that the girl had accepted a "pick-up" ride and lends support to the theory that it was a hit and run driver. However, there is still the possibility that the girl met some person she knew.

...A school chum thinks he saw her walking along the highway as he drove toward Canonsburg. But if this is true it was what she intended to do and thus far the information has not proved anything.

...Mary Iannarelli is dead, a victim of a peculiar incident – accident perhaps- and peculiar because of the subsequent circumstances. Perhaps she was the victim of somebody's ruthlessness, perhaps lust, yet more likely, because of somebody's misjudgment of distance or careless driving.

A young life, just budding into womanhood, has wilted and died, an insatiable desire for education and knowledge of the new land to which she was transported at an age which permitted her to contrast the old and appreciate the new. She wanted an education above all things and while getting it she was able to bring sunshine and happiness to her parents, reunited in this "promised land." She was a bright light and the ambitious spark of her home and a leader among her school, church and personal friends.

*Her life has been snuffed out just as it was budding into maturity?*
*(sic) Perhaps it was an accident and the transporting of the body*
*and the effort to conceal it might have been actuated by panic.*
*Police authorities and the family, hope that the perpetrator will*
*come forward, make a clean breast of the circumstances and help,*
*through honest effort, to clear up the mystery and give the family*
*the satisfaction of knowing what happened and how their*
*daughter died. Police believe that sooner or later the car driver*
*will come forward for his own sake, the sooner this is done the*
*better.*

*In the meantime Mary Iannarelli goes to her grave today, another*
*victim of highway carelessness — to say the least.*

*Funeral services for Miss Iannarelli were held this afternoon from*
*her late home at Muse in charge of Rev. John Kopera, pastor of St.*
*Mary's church at Cecil. Burial was in the St. Patrick's cemetery*
*here. Workers in the mine quit an hour earlier in order to*
*attend....(10)*

After the funeral, emotions were running high in Muse.
People who lived in the village were in disbelief over what had
occurred and were frustrated that nobody had yet been arrested
and charged with the crime. The rumors that circulated as truth
varied from the plausible to the ridiculous, but none were based
in fact. Feelings ran the strongest in the Italian community, who
had lost one of their own.

According to witnesses who were alive at the time, the
Italians gathered at the Muse Independent Club when they
weren't working. They talked and plotted actions that they could
take to speed the investigation along and bring the perpetrator
to justice. Some suggested that they go to the state police barracks *en masse* to protest the lack of results by the police. Others

spoke of how they would deal with the perpetrator once he was caught.

As frustrating as it was, they were all basically helpless as far as achieving a just result was concerned. Protests would not speed the investigation along, and would possibly slow it down. Discussions of doing harm to the person responsible were moot since they had nobody to attack. Although the story did not dominate the headlines in the *Daily Notes* for the first time since the incident, the paper ran an editorial on September 28, 1939 that attempted to quell the emotions that were running so high.

*A most regrettable Highway incident occurred here a few days ago which caused the death of a Cecil township high school girl. Whether it was a hit-and-run case or something more serious, is yet to be determined. State and county officers are seeking to unravel the mystery which surrounds the affair and the public joins in hoping that their investigation will be such as will clear up the case.*

*Officers have maintained a strict silence since the incident, last Saturday afternoon. Whether they have made any progress has not been revealed. They are zealously prosecuting the investigation, however.*

*In the meantime, public sentiment has reached a high point in indignation – and righteously so. However, all the stories that are circulating are not true. One should be careful about spreading this unconfirmed gossip because it might interfere with the orderly investigation made by officers and also bring innocent people under suspicion. Hardly any of the stories being circulated have any element of truth in them.*

*The common theory of the case is that the young girl was the victim of a hit-and-run driver, who, under the influence of panic loaded her into the car, presumably dead and hauled her to an isolated spot where she was placed under a parked car, in order to shift suspicion on the owner of the car.*

*Doubtless this driver has since regretted his rash act of the moment and would prefer to make a clean breast of the case and place himself on the mercy of the law for his action.*

*This would be the sensible thing to do, as sooner or later he will be found and the longer the delay, the more serious becomes the offense.*

*The state motor police officers have a reputation for getting their man and it is likely that he will be apprehended sooner or later, because his acts, no doubt, were on the spur of the moment and without premeditation with the result that his movements cannot continue to be kept secret.*

*Whoever he may be, wherever he may be, it would be wise to lose no time in righting the wrong and clearing up the case. (11)*

It is doubtful that the editorial completely quashed the cauldron of emotions in Muse. Ultimately there never were any protests at the state police barracks, and some of the more vocal protestations seemed to be mitigated. However, the undercurrent of frustration remained, and the case continued to be the main topic of conversation at the Muse Italian Club, as well as throughout the rest of the village.

One statement in the editorial that proved prescient regarded the state police officers who were investigating the crime. The family checked with them daily. The police never said much more, other than that they were working hard on the case and the family would be informed when they got a break. They continued to be completely tight-lipped about the progress of the investigation.

# CHAPTER 4

## AN ARREST IS MADE

—

FINALLY, nine days after the death of Mary Iannarelli, an arrest was made. To this day, it has never been revealed how the police were able to identify and finally arrest the perpetrator. All that is known is that the person responsible did not voluntarily surrender to police. Since there were no eyewitnesses to the crime, most surmised that the perpetrator told one too many people about what he had done and one of them turned him in. But if there was no hard evidence against him, there would have been no reason for the perpetrator to confess to his role in the crime as he did. This mystery was never resolved.

Once the arrest was announced, the story was once again on the front page of the *Daily Notes*. The headline for October 2, 1939, screamed:

### *LOCAL MAN HELD IN DEATH OF MUSE HIGH SCHOOL GIRL*

The sub-headlines and story went on to read:

*DOMINICK GUADAGNI OF EAST CANONSBURG*
*HELD TO AWAIT CORONER'S FINDING.*

**STORY IS TOLD**

## Accused Picks Up Ianarella (sic) Girl on Road
## – Leaps From Car to Death

### NO MOLESTATION

### Preliminary Hearing Held and Accused
### Committed Without Bail

Committed to the county jail on a technical charge of manslaughter and failing to stop to render assistance, is Dominick Guadagni, 616 Highland avenue, East Canonsburg, well known soccer football player and an employe (sic) of the Standard Tin Plate Company.

His arrest followed a week of relentless criminal investigation in the county – as a result of the death of Mary Iannarelli, 17(sic), of Muse, who was found under a parked car in Cecil township on Saturday afternoon, September 23.

She died in the Canonsburg General Hospital some hours later and since that time a man hunt has been under way in this section which has transcended all other news in the district....

Since then the manhunt has been under way and has never been abandoned for an hour until the book was closed and the confessed suspect was behind the bars in the county jail.

He had been arraigned before Justice of the Peace William D. Smith here, and held without bail on tentative charges of manslaughter and failing to stop to render assistance.

Coroner James B. Jones announced last night that no date for an inquest has been set as yet, due to two other violent death cases on his caledar (sic) which will be disposed of before this case is taken up. It is likely the inquest will be the latter part of the week.

The arrest of Guadagni was the result of the tireless work of two members of the Pennsylvania Motor Police, Corporal George H. Benson and Private J. R. Fair, together with Chief County Detective M. J. Powell. In winding up his case Corporal Benson *gave acknowledgement to the cooperation and services of Chief of Police Harold Addis and Lieut. Walter Miller of the Canonsburg borough police department, who have been working with the state and county offices since the finding of the girl's body and who have rendered valuable assistance.*

*Placed under arrest while at work at the Standard plant, Guadagni denied his guilt and continued to deny it until Saturday evening, when he capitulated and made a full confession,* **or at least told his version of the story.** *(Author's emphasis)*

## Girl "Picked Up"

*In substance, he told the officers that he was driving out the Valley Road on that Saturday afternoon and that he offered the girl a ride. She accepted and entered the car, but instead of going immediately to her home at Muse, he turned off on what is known as the Engle road near the mine of the Chartiers Gas Coal Company commonly called the "Springer Mine".*

*The story, as told by the accused man, was that he drove about a mile out the Engle road and then turned off on the Hickman school house road.*

## Leaps From Car

*Just as he was driving past the Frank Adams home near which McConnell has his garden, the girl without provocation or warning, jumped from the car, the confession said. She struck the red dog\* road and rolled under the McConnell car, Guadagni stated. He added that he slowed down and prepared to stop, then becoming panic stricken, he hurried away without stopping and returned to his home by a roundabout route.*

*Since that time he has sought to keep his secret.*

## Mystery is Solved

How the state police officers were able to get the clues that led to the arrest of the suspect who proved to be the guilty man, will never be known. That part of the investigation is a sealed book for the records of the department and will not be made public.

Suffice, the officers started with nothing and completed their case in just a week.

## Bitter Feeling at Muse

In the Muse community feeling has been running high and dire threats have been made by the hundreds of miners who are employed there, who live there and who work with the girl's father and brother and whose children have gone to school with the victim of the affair.

Their indignation has been such that the officers made nothing known of the progress of their investigation and after Guadagni's arrest and subsequent confession, no announcement was made and he was slipped here quietly for a preliminary hearing and then committed to the county jail without any news of his arrest getting circulated. They feared the temper of the Muse miners would break loose and a more serious situation might develop.

> (*Note: Red dog is a byproduct of the coal mining process. It is a mixture of slate, rock and other impurities that are separated from the coal after cleaning. It was often used as a road surfacing material on dirt roads in the 20th century in Western Pennsylvania.)

## Accused Is Married Man

Guadagni is 30 years of age and is married and has one child. At this time however, he is separated from his wife it is understood and has been staying at the home of his parents.

*His arrest brought surprise to many in this community due to the prominence of his family and the respect in which they are held in the East End section. No member of the family had any knowledge of the affair, it is understood, their first intimation that Dominick was suspected coming with his arrest.*

## No Criminal Attack

*The state police and Coroner James B. Jones announced today that there was no indication that a criminal assault had been made or attempted upon the girl. An autopsy was performed which established this fact and other circumstances convinced the officers that the girl had not been criminally molested.*

*This however, does not lessen the indignation of the community where the girl has resided since she was brought from the place of her birth, in Italy, five (sic) years ago, and transplanted to Muse, where she has since resided, where she went from the third grade to the eighth grade in school in one year and where she has been an honor student for several years. In 1937 she was awarded the American Legion Auxiliary medal for the greatest scholarship attainment for the current year.*

## Popular in School

*She was a favorite with school authorities and schoolmates as well as in the immediate community where she lived.*

*The officers stated today that they hope the quick cleanup of the case will serve to lessen the tension in Muse and that the case will take its orderly way through the courts where justice will be done – in the manner setup by law. (12)*

At this point, Mary's family and the Muse community were stunned by the arrest of Guadagni. Speculation immediately started as to how Mary ended up in the car with Guadagni and what really happened to her on that lonely road. Even more disconcerting to the Italian community was that one of their own, albeit from Canonsburg and not Muse, had committed the crime.

One of the first glaring discrepancies in Guadagni's story was his allegation that he was travelling on Valley Rd., offered Mary a ride, and then made a turn onto Engle (Burnside) Road. If he really was on Valley Rd. he would have driven straight across Rte. 980 to get onto Burnside Rd. Mary would have been walking along Rte. 980 as that would have been the most direct route to Muse from the Pacifico home in east Canonsburg. There was no possible way for Guadagni to make a turn onto Burnside Rd. from Valley Rd.

View from Valley Road Across Rte. 980 to Burnside (Engle) Road

Furthermore, the elapsed time of only 15 – 20 minutes between her leaving the Pacifico house and her body being found by McConnell would be impossible. If Guadagni was travelling on Valley Road as he stated before he picked Mary up, she would have had to have already walked more than one mile from the Pacifico home to the intersection of Rte.980 with Burnside Rd. and Valley Rd. She then would have been picked up near the end of Valley Rd., driven to the McConnell site, been assaulted and left for dead in a total of 15 -20 minutes. It is much more likely that Guadagni was driving somewhere near the Pacifico home in Canonsburg when he picked her up, which would have allowed sufficient time for all the subsequent events to take place. This was also the only scenario where he would have had to make a turn onto Burnside Road as he stated. Why this discrepancy was never questioned remains a mystery. One could speculate that either the police were incompetent or were covering up the magnitude of the crime for some unknown reason.

One of the strange coincidences of the case was the address of Guadagni's residence. He resided only a few doors up Highland Avenue in Canonsburg from the business of Frank DiPoala, the man who provided Mary a ride to Canonsburg earlier that fateful day. Furthermore, his home was only a few blocks from the Pacifico house, a fact which makes his story that he was travelling on Valley Rd. even more suspect.

The story continued to dominate the headlines the next day, October 3, 1939.

### Ianarelli Case Interest Goes On
#### Inquest Date Not Set Yet
CORONER JONES NOT READY HE STATES
- ACCUSED WILL NOT BE CALLED

### BLOOMS ENGAGED
GUADAGNI GOES TO WORLD'S FAIR FEW HOURS
AFTER FATAL INCIDENT

*While police authorities worked today to clean up the remaining loose ends in the death of Mary Ianarelli, 17 year-old Muse high*

*school girl who allegedly leaped to her death from the car of
Dominick Guadagni of Canonsburg on Saturday, September 23,,
the latter, accused of manslaughter and failure to stop and
render assistance, was being held without bail in the
Washington county jail.*

*No further important developments seem likely to appear until
the inquest which Coroner James B. Jones said will be held next
week in the Washington court house. Guadagni, he said, would
probably not be called to appear at the inquest.*

*The law firm of Bloom and Bloom of Washington, it is understood,
has been retained as counsel for the young man. Both members of
this firm were out of town today and could not be contacted to
verify this report.*

*There were several hitherto undisclosed developments in the case
today. Most important was the fact that the victim of he (sic)
tragedy had not been unconscious the entire time between the
discovery of her body under an automobile on the Hickman
school house road and her death at the Canonsburg General
hospital some time later, as previously believed. Exactly what she
said the few periods when rationality apparently returned was not
disclosed, but authorities said that some of her words were
intelligible and coherent.*

*Another interesting sidelight on the case developed today. Only a
few hours after the fatal tragedy Guadagni boarded an excursion
train here for New York City, to attend the World's Fair. If the
events of that afternoon preyed on his mind, the young man gave
no evidence of it, according to another passenger. He and some
friends trooped through the cars, apparently in gay, high spirits.
He returned to this city after a day in New York. (13)*

If Guadagni felt any remorse for his role in Mary's death, his
actions certainly did not show it. Anyone who could leave

another person for dead and then board an overnight train to attend a fair indicates a sociopathic personality.

**Dominick Guadagni**

Another incident that showed a complete lack of remorse occurred several days after the incident, but before Guadagni's arrest. It was reported by a witness (Ralph Cheverine, now deceased) that Guadagni was drinking and playing cards at a bar on Third Street (now Perry Como Avenue ) in East Canonsburg. The main topic of conversation there, as it was everywhere in the region, was the situation surrounding the death of Mary Iannarelli. It was reported that Guadagni appeared as shocked and mystified by recent events as all of the other people at the bar that day. He was heard to make a statement to the effect, "Whoever did that, the SOB should be tarred and feathered". It was as though he had completely disassociated himself from his role in the events of that day.

# CHAPTER 5

## INQUEST AND HEARING

—

NEWSPAPER reports of new developments disappeared until the October 16, 1939 edition of the *Daily Notes* recounted the activities of the coroner's inquest.

### *Guadagni Held for Involuntary Manslaughter at Inquest*
#### **Appears at Hearing This Morning; Does Not Testify**
##### SIGNED STATEMENT OF LOCAL MAN READ
##### BY STATE POLICE OFFICER

#### *BOND AT $5,000*
##### PRISONER CLAIMS MARY IANARELLI
##### LEAPED TO DEATH WITHOUT WARNING

*A coroner's jury meeting in the grand jury room of the court house with no previous announcement recommended this morning that Dominick Guadagni, 30, of 616 Highland avenue, Canonsburg, be held on a charge of involuntary manslaughter for the death of Mary Ianarelli, 17-year-old Cecil high school student.*

*The inquest called by Coroner James B. Jones was not open to the public. It lasted for only a few minutes, Private John Fair of the state motor police being the only witness called. The jury, of which W. D. McCarrell, Tylerdale justice of the peace, was foreman, returned its verdict in less than 10 minutes.*

## Girl Died Sept. 23

*Public interest has been high in this case ever since the body of
Mary Ianarelli was found by Thomas McConnell under his
parked car on the Hickman school house road in Cecil township
on the afternoon of September 23. Guadagni was arrested a week
later and told police that the girl had jumped from his car after he
had offered her a ride.*

*After a preliminary hearing here before Justice of the Peace
William D. Smith at which Guadagni was held for court on a
charge of involuntary manslaughter and failure to stop and render
assistance, he was taken to the Washington county jail where he
has been held ever since. Bail has been set by Judge Carl E.
Gibson at $5,000.*

## Guadagni Present at Inquest

*Guadagni was present at the inquest this morning, accompanied
by his counsel, I. C. Bloom. He did not testify.*

*Private Fair's testimony consisted entirely of a reading of the
statement which Guadagni signed following his arrest here.*

*According to this testimony Guadagni was driving out the Valley
Road toward Muse on the afternoon of Saturday, September 23.
He saw the Ianarelli girl walking along the highway and offered
her a ride which she accepted. When Guadagni reached the
Hickman school house road he turned off and* **when Miss
Ianarelli asked where they were going he replied that they were
"going for a ride"**. *(Author's emphasis)*

## Jumped Without Warning

*Without any warning, he claims, the girl jumped from the car
which at that time was going about 20 miles an hour. Guadagni
said that he slowed down slightly, then continued without looking*

*back to see what had happened to the girl. He went home, dressed, and early that evening took an excursion train to the World's Fair in New York City, he said.*

*Private Fair was questioned briefly by Attorney Bloom, but added no important testimony.*

*The coroner's office now has concluded its part in the case, Coroner Jones said, and all evidence will be turned over to the office of the district attorney. It is likely that the case will be presented at the next session of the grand jury which convenes on November 6. (14)*

Forensic science and criminal investigation in 1939 were not what they are today and the same holds true for neurosurgery. Had this event taken place even a few years later, Mary Iannarelli would have likely survived the ordeal. She probably would have been impaired in some way but she most likely would have survived. Many surgical advancements and treatments that were not available before World War II were developed shortly thereafter. As it was, doctors performed no surgery or pressure relief on the brain, and she died approximately twelve hours after her injuries were incurred.

Coincidentally, her brother, Robert, sustained a similar injury in 1979 when he was involved in a workplace accident. The side of his skull was crushed in an eerily similar manner as Mary's injury. Thanks to rapid evacuation and transportation, and a skilled neurosurgeon who performed a nine-hour surgery, his life was saved. He lived on with only slight impairment to indicate what he had suffered. Had his treatment been the same as his sister's, their outcomes would most likely have been the same.

It appears from the newspaper reports that by the date of the coroner's inquest, the police had put the entire investigation behind them. They clearly were taking the approach that they had nabbed the perpetrator, he had confessed, and the case was closed. They appeared to take Guadagni's version at face value without accounting for the discrepancies, exploring other scenarios, or delving deeper into the unanswered questions.

It was never reported if Guadagni's car had been searched for a weapon that could have been used to inflict the injury to Mary's head. If he did hit her with something in the car, he most likely would have disposed of it, but a cursory search of the vehicle may have shed more light on the mystery. It was also never reported whether his car had ever been searched for blood splatter, which would have proven that an assault had taken place in the car.

The original police theory of what took place sheds light on the ineptitude of the investigation. As reported in the *Daily Notes*, the police first theorized that there was no foul play since it had been at most twenty minutes between the time Mary had left the Pacifico house and her body was found more than two miles away. Logic would indicate quite the opposite. According to the Pacificos, she left their home and intended to walk to Muse. Since she was found several miles from where she was last seen, the only way that she could have ended up under the McConnell car in twenty minutes was if she had been driven there. If she was driven there, then obviously something nefarious had to have taken place because it would have been impossible to walk that distance in the time available.

The police also initially theorized that Mary had been struck by a car somewhere near where she was found. They surmised that the person responsible had then stopped, placed her body in his car, and transported the body to the McConnell site to make it look like McConnell had struck the girl. This makes no sense at all. Why a law enforcement official would even propose it leaves many questions as to their abilities or motives. If someone were to strike another person with a car, intending to make it look like a hit-and-run accident, especially along a seldom travelled country road, the sensible thing to do would be to leave the body where it lay and drive off. There is no logical reason why a person would stop, lift the dead weight into the car (not to mention causing possible blood stains to the inside of the car), drive several miles, and then remove the body to place it under another car.

Another mystery is how she ended up in Guadagni's car to begin with. It is unlikely that her parents were wrong about her never willingly accepting a ride from a stranger if offered. Others who knew her well also believed as her parents did that she would never accept a ride from someone unknown to her. It is possible that she did know Guadagni and hence accepted the ride. However, since she was a high school student from Muse and Guadagni was a 30 year old married factory worker from Canonsburg the scenario would be highly unlikely. Nobody else in the family had ever heard of Dominick Guadagni until this incident, so there is no reason to conclude that she might have somehow known him.

Mary may have been feeling tired, or could have been experiencing some sort of discomfort that would have caused her to accept a ride. However, doctors' examinations at Canonsburg General Hospital verified that she had suffered nothing other than the head wound, which would negate the likelihood that she was injured in some way that caused her to get into the car.

The most likely scenario is that an attractive, teenaged girl walking alone along a highway was too great a temptation for a thirty year-old man who was separated from his wife. Guadagni possibly forced her into his car by brandishing a weapon, or simply grabbed her and pushed her inside. Either way, once she was in the car, he probably began to make advances and when she refused, he bludgeoned her. This is all still speculation about what may have happened but in retrospect, it is the most likely scenario.

Imagine the horror that a young girl would have felt if she were coerced into a car by an adult male who turned down a country road, away from the direction of her home and safety, and said, "We're going for a ride", as per Guadagni's own admission. Although the coroner stated that no sexual assault had taken place, it is rather obvious from the known facts that Guadagni's intentions were nefarious. If the police ever questioned Guadagni's meaning and intent that they "were going for a ride," it was never made public. If they did not question what he meant, it would be another indication of how inept or biased the police must have been. If he did not have any ulterior motives, he would have driven straight to Muse instead of taking her "for a ride".

The most glaring discrepancy in Guadagni's story is that Mary jumped from his car while travelling at twenty miles per hour down a dirt road. According to the perpetrator, she struck the ground, rolled some distance, and came to rest behind the McConnell car. There were two relevant statements from the original police investigation cited earlier from the September 25, 1939 edition of the *Daily Notes*.

*...then carried her body several miles to an isolated spot on a back road, placed it (the body) carefully under the wheels of another car*

*A purse and some dress goods which she had purchased in Canonsburg were lying at her side (15)*

The September 26 edition of the *Daily Notes* contained the following telling statement:

*........She had made several small purchases while here, one of them some dress goods. This was found near her body when she was discovered under the McConnell car. Also her purse, containing something over 30 cents, was under the car, indicating that the **person or persons who placed her body there were meticulous about the details, leaving nothing behind.** Author's emphasis (16)*

The fact that the police believed that the body was "placed carefully under the wheels of another car" and "the person or persons who placed her body there were meticulous about the details" would certainly imply that the scene had been staged. If the scene was not staged, it would have been highly unlikely that she would have rolled some distance, come to rest under the wheels of another car, and then end with the appearance of having been placed there.

The second statement disproves Guadagni's story even further. If she leapt from the car and rolled down the hill before coming to rest, we would have to believe that her purse and dress goods would have slid down the same trajectory and conveniently come to rest lying by her side. The probability of the body and two other objects ending up side by side and some distance away after leaving a car that was going twenty miles per hour is virtually zero. Based on their own findings and preliminary conclusions that the body had been carefully placed under the McConnell car, it is incomprehensible that the police would accept Guadagni's story that Mary had leapt from the car and landed where and how she did.

Also recall that it was reported in the September 25, 1939, edition of the *Daily Notes* that,

> *"although the road between the spot where she was last seen and where she was found, has been gone over foot by foot, no trace of an accident could be found."*

If she did jump, then certainly some disruption to the loose dirt and red dog near where she was found would have been apparent to the searchers. In the same edition, it was reported by McConnell, *"Notifying the officers, he awaited their arrival without touching the body or his car and without disturbing the dust of the road."* If the dirt was undisturbed and showed no evidence of fall from a moving car, then the alleged leap had to be fictitious.

The final and most important fact that discredits Guadagni's version of events is that there were no injuries to Mary's body other than to the left side of her head. In addition, her clothes were reported to be clean and unsoiled in any way. That begs the question as to how someone could leap from a moving vehicle onto a red dog road, strike the ground, roll some distance, and then not have any scrapes, scratches, or bruises, or have any dirt or damage done to her clothing.

The investigation of inconsistencies seems so fundamental to good police work that it is preposterous that they were not looked into further. As was reported in the October 16, 1939, *Daily Notes* and quoted earlier, Private Fair's entire testimony at the coroner's inquest was a reading of the prepared statement that had been signed by Guadagni. He never mentioned an on-going investigation nor did he mention any discrepancies in the signed statement. They clearly wanted to put the case behind them once they received the confession. The police based their entire case on the word of the person who had the most to lose by telling the truth. More speculation might lead one to believe that the police could have even coached Guadagni's confession in order to mitigate further investigation.

Since no sexual assault could be proven, one could surmise it was most likely a result of Mary's actions to defend herself. If she was forced into the car, she would have realized immediately that she was in trouble. If she got into the car voluntarily, she would have quickly reached the same conclusion when the driver turned down a dirt road and told her that they were "going for a ride." What could any teenaged girl conclude would happen if she were in a car with a strange adult man who proceeded to drive further and further into the country in the wrong direction? Remember, Guadagni was allegedly providing her a ride home. The way home was to continue on Rte.980 toward Muse. It was not to turn down Engle Rd. (Burnside Rd.) and then turn again on Hickman Schoolhouse Road (Angerer Rd.)

There are two likely possibilities about what happened that day. The first is that somewhere along Hickman Schoolhouse Road, Guadagni stopped the car and began making advances, which Mary protested and perhaps even fought. The second is that when Mary saw that she was being driven further and further from her intended destination, she realized what was happening and became combative. Guadagni would have then stopped the car and attempted to overcome her to keep from getting caught. He may have realized that if she got away at that point, he would have a difficult time explaining his actions. To that end, he would have grabbed an object inside the car and struck her on the side of the head. Since she would have been in the passenger seat when he struck her, it would have been on the left side of her head, the actual location of her injury. Had she really leapt from the passenger side of the car, it is much more likely that she would have struck the right side of her head, not the left. In order to strike the left side of her head while exiting the passenger side of a moving car, she would have had to rotate more than a hundred and eighty degrees in the air while falling.

Once Guadagni saw what he had done inside his car, he made the decision to dump the body in a convenient location away from his vehicle. He spotted the parked McConnell car and no witnesses nearby. He then removed the comatose body from the car, placed it under the McConnell car along with her purse and shopping goods, and drove away. He was hoping to implicate the owner of the parked car so that he could drive away scot-free.

While this is certainly speculative, circumstantial evidence is based on speculation and logic and is acceptable in a court of law. Guadagni's story of what happened that day so many years ago is completely unreliable because it not only stretches what's believable, but is completely self-serving. The family of Mary Iannarelli always believed that there was more to the story and that Guadagni had committed murder, not manslaughter. Their protestations to the police fell upon deaf ears. The fact that they were immigrants and did not have command of the English language or understood the American judicial system may have played a role. The police were satisfied that they got their man and the specific charges placed against him by the prosecutors seemed irrelevant to them.

Like all news stories, this one had run its cycle. There was not much to report now that Mary was buried and the person responsible for her death sat in the county jail. On November 10, Guadagni was arraigned once again. Although still a front-page story in the *Daily Notes*, it was no longer a headline, and this article began in the middle of the page.

### GUADAGNI HELD TO ANSWER FOR DEATH OF GIRL
#### East End Man arraigned in Justice Court Today and Returned to Jail

*Arraigned before Justice of the Peace W. D. Smith, this morning, Dominick Guadagni, of Highland avenue was held for action of the grand jury on a charge of involuntary manslaughter growing out of the death on Saturday, September 23 of Mary Ianarella (sic), of Muse. No bail was fixed and at the conclusion of the brief hearing he was returned to the Washington county jail.*

*On two additional charges, failing to stop after an accident to render assistance, and for hit-and-run, his attorneys Bloom & Bloom waived hearing....*

*Corporal Benson read the statement purported to have been made by Guadagni after his arrest and no other evidence was produced....(17)*

The story made the front page of the *Daily Notes* again on November 16, 1939 when Guadagni was indicted by a grand jury.

### Jury Finds True Bill Against Guadagni
#### TRIAL IS SET FOR NOVEMBER 21
#### Local Young Man Faces Probable Maximum Sentence Of Three Years

## *INTEREST HIGH*

### Charges Grow Out of Death of Mary Ianarelli, Muse High School Girl

*Dominick Guadagni of Canonsburg was indicted by the grand jury in Washington this morning on a charge of involuntary manslaughter after the same body yesterday afternoon returned a true bill against the local young man on a charge of failure to stop after an accident and failure to disclose his identity. Both charges grow out of the death of Mary Ianarelli, 17-year old Muse high school girl, who Guadagni said leapt from his automobile while he was taking her for a ride. Trial date on both indictments was set for Tuesday, November 21.*

*Both charges pending against the local young man carry a maximum sentence of three years. Where a defendant is found guilty on both counts, it is customary to have the sentence run concurrently. If this procedure is followed by the court, Guadagni faces a maximum sentence of three years should he be found guilty....(18)*

# CHAPTER 6

## THE SENTENCE

—

AT this point, the family was in a state of disbelief that three years would be the maximum sentence that Guadagni could have had imposed on him. How could someone who was directly responsible for the death of their daughter/sister basically get away with what they believed to be murder? At some level, they still hoped that when the trial was concluded with a guilty verdict that Guadagni would be sent to prison for a much longer period of time. Little did they know that the coming months would bring even worse news. Their faith in the American justice system faltered. The family, their friends, and co-workers at the Muse Mine were astonished at this pending miscarriage of justice. The main topic of discussion most days at the Muse Italian Club was their disgust with the judicial system.

Any hope that the matter would reach a speedy resolution was soon proven to be unfounded optimism. Five days after the grand jury handed down their indictment, the *Daily Notes* reported a story on November 21, 1939, about the large number of criminal cases awaiting trial in Washington.

## *CRIMINAL TERM COMES TO END; DOCKET HEAVY*
### Many Cases to be Carried Over To Special Term or to February Session

*That the trial of Dominick Guadagni held for manslaughter, failure to reveal identity and failure to stop to render assistance in the death of Mary Ianarilla (sic), of Muse may not be heard at this term of the criminal court, became apparent today.*

*Tomorrow is the last day for the regular term of criminal court and there are something like 50 to 60 cases remaining for trial....*

*That it is likely that a special term of criminal court may be called in January, to dispose of the accumulation is advanced by many attorneys and court observers....(19)*

It should be noted for future significance that Guadagni was in jail during this entire time. He was unable to post the five thousand dollar bond imposed by the court after his initial arrest, so he remained incarcerated in the Washington County jail.

Once again any thoughts of a January trial date proved to be wishful thinking. The local news was silent on the matter until the February 13, 1940, edition of the *Daily Notes* hit the newsstands. Once again, the story was front page news.

### *Guadagni Trial is on Court List*
#### CASE WHICH ATTRACTED MUCH ATTENTION
#### TO BE HEARD ON FEBRUARY 23
#### HELD IN JAIL

*With 85 cases listed for trial during the session, criminal court was started in Washington today and will continue throughout the month with the three judges urging speed consistent with the proper time for presentation to the end that the docket may be cleared at the earliest date.*

*Two cases of more than ordinary interest here are scheduled for Friday, February 23. They are those of Dominick Guadagni, of Canonsburg, charged with involuntary manslaughter in the death of Mary Ianarelli, of Muse and also with failing to stop after an accident, to render assistance....(20)*

Any thoughts that the case would finally reach a just resolution were quickly quashed; the latest continuance postponed the trial until spring. The family continued to hope that something would be revealed at the trial that would shed more light onto what really happened that fateful day in September. Loaded court dockets and continuances added more fuel to the frustration felt by everyone worried about the outcome of the case. The trial was ultimately moved to May 2, 1940.

Greater insults were yet to come. Upon the advice of his attorneys, Guadagni chose to simply plead guilty to the charges before him. By doing so, he avoided a trial and also dodged more questions being brought up concerning his actions on September 23, 1939. Guadagni went to his hearing, pleaded guilty, and threw himself at the mercy of the court.

At this hearing, Mary's brother, Robert, attempted to assault Guadagni in the courtroom, but was restrained by the bailiff and sheriff's deputies. Robert continued to publicly make threats against Guadagni for several months after the hearing. The powers that be could not stand idly by and tolerate a potential troublemaker. Even though he was not a US citizen, Robert was rewarded for his loyalty to his sister by being drafted into the US Army in 1940. Other than a short leave in November, 1941, he did not return home again for over three years. He was finally discharged in 1945. Most of those years were spent in the South Pacific Theater of operations, and also included one year as a prisoner of war of the empire of Japan. He was finally discharged in 1945. By then, Guadagni had already been in California for several years and out of the reach of anyone who may have had revenge on their mind.

Robert - 1939

For whatever reason, the judge did not even impose the maximum sentence allowed for the charges. The last mention of the entire sordid affair appeared in the May 2, 1940, edition of the *Daily Notes*.

### Guadagni Gets One to 3 Years

*Dominick Guadagni, East Canonsburg young man, was today sentenced to serve one to three years in the county jail on a charge of involuntary manslaughter and one year to the county jail for failure to stop and render assistance after an accident.*

*He was before the court on a request to plead guilty to charges growing out of the death of Mary Ianarelli, 18, of Muse. The girl's body was found under a car on an isolated back road in Cecil township Sept. 23, 1939. She died 12 hours later in the Canonsburg hospital.*

*The defendant, who has been in custody since one week after the death of the girl, pleaded guilty to failure to stop after the accident and concealing his identity and on the charge of manslaughter. The case was submitted to the court on a statement of facts and the court found him guilty and the sentences were pronounced. They are to run concurrently.*

*The court held that the defendant had shown gross negligence in his failure to stop when the girl jumped from the car and because of this negligence the court held that he was guilty of manslaughter.*

*The death of Mary Ianarelli and the subsequent arrest and confession of the man responsible for the fatal accident was one of the most sensational cases in this district in recent years. Public opinion was inflamed in the days after the high school girl's broken body was found abandoned along the road, and the developments of the case were followed with avid interest.*

*In confessing his part in the fatality, Guadagni claimed that she had jumped from the car of her own volition. He admitted offering her a ride to her home as she was walking along the road. When he turned off the main route, the girl, he said, jumped from the machine. He told police that he continued without stopping to see whether she had been injured. (21)*

Reading the last paragraph would lead one to believe that Mary had allegedly jumped shortly after the car left the main road to Muse. In reality, it was almost two miles from the highway. That would be plenty of time for her to learn about Guadagni's true intentions. The only evidence that Mary allegedly jumped is Guadagni's word, which is highly suspicious as people ordinarily do not jump from a moving automobile without a motive. It also defies logic to allege that Mary would have gotten into the car voluntarily and then jumped out of the same moving car for no reason several minutes later.

Just like people will jump from a burning building to escape being burned alive, the same thought process would apply to a person who jumps from a moving car. If she did jump, then something was going on inside that car that led her to believe that jumping was a better alternative than to remain in the car. In Guadagni's mind, his story about the alleged jump from the car probably would provide a more favorable outcome for him than what really happened. He was right.

The family was shocked with the result of the hearing. Most people felt that the maximum sentence of three years was not enough for the magnitude of the crime. They were now outraged with the sentence of one to three years. They believed that Guadagni had gotten away with murder and if not murder, at the very least his criminal actions caused a series of events to transpire that led to her death. Either way, he was responsible. One to three years amounted to a slap on the wrist.

After the May 2 pronouncement, any satisfaction that the family derived from knowing that Guadagni was safely ensconced in the county jail for one to three years was quickly dispelled. Shortly before the one-year anniversary of his arrest on October 2, Guadagni was released by the court from his jail cell. He was given credit for time served since the day of his arrest and he was free to do as he pleased.

The outrage was palpable, and talk in the Muse Italian Club centered on taking justice into their own hands. In their minds, Guadagni was responsible for Mary Iannarelli's death. The police and the American justice system had failed, and as far as the family and the people of Muse were concerned, Guadagni had gotten away with murder. There was no legitimacy in Guadagni serving less than one year in the relative luxury of the county jail as a fair trade for a young girl's life. In the minds of the police and the law, justice had been served. The guilty party had been apprehended and he had paid his debt to society. Unfortunately for the family, there were no other avenues to appeal for further recrimination.

# CHAPTER 7

## AFTERMATH

—

ANY faith in God disappeared in Carlo and Irene's mind over the circumstances surrounding the loss of their daughter. They could not understand how God could allow this to happen to an innocent young girl and how He could let the guilty party essentially walk away. They gave up their Catholic faith, and to the best of anyone's knowledge, never set foot in a church for the rest of their lives.

In 1941, Carlo and Irene decided to leave Muse and move to Canonsburg. The home where they resided in Muse held too many memories of the daughter they no longer had. The memory that made it most intolerable was of Mary lying in her coffin in the family living room. The other and more important reason for the move to Canonsburg was to be closer to their daughter's grave. They purchased a home on East College Street and resided there until their own deaths many years later.

Carlo continued to work at the Muse Mine until it closed in 1954. He rode the I. C. Patch bus back and forth to Muse every day that he worked. After the mine closed, he put his carpentry skills to work with a construction crew building homes for a local contractor. His health was such that he was able to work well into his eighties.

Life continued in their new home. Carlo and Irene put a large garden in the back-yard of their home every spring. When the vegetables were ready in the fall, Irene canned most of the harvest. Wine-making time arrived with the falling leaves of autumn, and the trip in someone's truck to Pittsburgh to buy the grapes was always a day to look forward to. Sausage and prosciutto hung in the basement over the winter. Life took on the rhythm of the seasons, but was always haunted by the hole in their lives created by the loss of their daughter. New Year's Day was not a day of celebration anymore as it would always be Mary's birthday. Likewise, September 24 was always a solemn occasion as it marked the anniversary of her death. Far-away looks that often appeared on their faces bore witness to the continuing torment taking place in their minds.

Almost every Sunday after the traditional Italian family dinner, Robert drove Irene to St. Patrick's Cemetery to visit Mary's grave. When weather permitted, fresh flowers were planted on the grave, providing a proliferation of color. The grave was one of the prettiest in the entire cemetery. The head-stone itself was made of white marble that caused it to stand out and be clearly visible among the gray granite stones. A picture of Mary was centered on the headstone, and the entire grave was outlined in a six-inch wide strip of white marble. Such was Irene's determination to tend the grave that there were occasions where she walked the approximate two miles from her home to the cemetery to make sure that all was in order. Except for the days that brought inclement weather, she did this every Sunday until her death at the age of eighty six.

Guadagni left for California shortly after his release. The notoriety of what he had done precluded a peaceful existence in Canonsburg. His safety was also in question as there were many people who thought openly of evening the score. There is no record whether he ever returned to Canonsburg.

Guadagni died of cancer on April 13, 1955, at the age of forty six. Word quickly got back to Canonsburg of his demise. Although there were no open celebrations of his death by the Iannarelli family, there was relief that their daughter's killer was finally dead himself. It was a pyrrhic victory at best, but a victory nonetheless. Because he died at a relatively young age and had probably suffered before passing, they felt that justice had finally been served. The object of their scorn was finally gone.

# EPILOGUE

ALL of the main characters in this story are now deceased. Irene and Carlo are buried together in a newer section of St. Patrick's Cemetery. Robert and his wife, also named Mary, are buried nearby. The grave of the victim of this story is in one of the oldest sections of the cemetery.

She lies alone and about half a mile apart from the people who knew and loved her best. Today her grave has suffered the effects of time and inattention. The sparkling white headstone is now gray and no longer stands apart from all of the others nearby. Mary's picture is gone from the front of the headstone, as is the marble outline of the grave. The grave is grown over with grass and shows no evidence of the proliferation of flowers that were once always present. The only maintenance done is by the mowers who cut the grass that has grown over the grave.

Mary's Headstone

On my infrequent visits to Canonsburg, I always make an attempt to visit the family graves in St. Patrick's Cemetery. As I do with all the graves, I also place flowers on Mary's grave. These are probably the only flowers placed there in more than thirty years. The memory of her is slowly fading into history, and with each passing year and each new generation of descendants she is becoming less and less a part of the family story. Most know nothing of her existence or how she met such an unfortunate end. She will soon be just a name and two dates on a headstone in a forgotten corner of St. Patrick's Cemetery.

You have undoubtedly surmised by now that this is a part of my family story. Carlo and Irene were my grandparents, Robert was my father, and Mary was my aunt. I was born six years after her untimely death. I never knew her, but grew up hearing countless tales of the wonderful young woman she had become. You can rest in peace now Mary; your story has been told. You will never be forgotten.

*Bob Ianarelli*

# AFTERWORD

MARY'S story has been in my mind ever since I became old enough to understand that someone who was very dearly loved was missing from my family. As I grew older I became more sensitive and aware of the terrible loss that was felt by my grandparents when Mary was killed. As a young, impressionable boy, I frequently accompanied my father and grandmother for the weekly graveside visits. I witnessed the care that Irene took in placing the flowers at her grave. I also witnessed the tears that were frequently shed. "Why" was always the word that preceded any discussion of what had transpired and it is the one question that has no answer no matter how many times it is asked.

In a seven-year span commencing in 1984, Irene, Robert, and Carlo, all passed away. The tender loving care that had been given to Mary's gravesite ceased to be. The long, slow slide into neglect and disrepair began. I left Canonsburg for college in 1963. Other than summer vacations and other school breaks during the next four years, and for a few months in 1972, I was never a resident of Canonsburg again. My career took me to several locations in the United States. Like most people, the process of living and raising a family of my own took precedent over childhood memories. However, Mary's story was always firmly ensconced in a corner of my mind.

Several years ago, I decided to undertake the task of putting this story in writing. It has proceeded in fits and starts with at least two visits to the Frank Sarris Library in Canonsburg to research the *Daily Notes* news items and other sources from all those years ago. It also included a visit to Barisciano along the way to get a feel of the town from which my family had sprung. The corona-virus and home quarantine finally provided the impetus to complete the task at hand. My own advancing age provided a "now or never" urgency.

I hope that I have conveyed the family history and the story of Mary's death in a manner that the readers will find engaging. It was a labor of love that the future generations of Carlo and Irene's descendants can reference for a small, sad piece of their family's story. Others can look upon it as a tragedy but also a unique piece of local history that took place in a simpler time in Western Pennsylvania.

I would like to thank my Aunt Lena Nackoul and Uncle Harry Leonardi (both now deceased) who were both about Mary's age at the time of her death. They provided a lot of the background on Muse and how the events that transpired affected the community. I would also like to thank my wife, Jean. She accompanied me on my research visits to the library and on all my visits to St. Patrick's Cemetery. A visit to Barisciano several years ago provided both of us with a real educational experience in Italy.

I also have to thank Linda Layburn Secrest. She was my muse and editor in absentia. She provided invaluable insights regarding all the things that make a story flow and enjoyable to read as well as some guidance with publishing. Jennie Horn also reviewed the first draft and provided several suggestions for improvement. Who would have ever predicted when we entered first grade as innocent children at the North Central School in

Canonsburg in 1951 that we would be collaborating on a writing project almost seventy years later?

Others who provided input were my friend from cradle to grave, Dennis Colusci, and my cousin, Maria Teresa D'Alessandro in Barisciano, Italy. She welcomed us into her home and her genealogical research on my behalf proved invaluable. My daughter, Monica Ianarelli, helped with editing and provided photographic assistance for some of the locations discussed in the book. The Jefferson College Historical Society's research on my behalf uncovered several relevant articles that I had not seen before. Patty Burnside Quigley, a classmate from Canon-McMillan High School, and her friend, Lee Jones, helped to clarify the change in road names that have taken place since 1939. Finally, my son-in-law, Pasquale Vittori provided many valuable insights into Italian history.

Thank you everyone.

# NOTES

(1) Daily Notes, September 27, 1939, p.2

(2) Ibid

(3) Daily Notes, September 25, 1939, p.3

(4) Daily Notes, September 27, 1939, p.2

(5) Ibid

(6) Daily Notes, September 25, 1939, p.3

(7) Daily Notes, September 27, 1939, p.3

(8) Daily Notes, September 25, 1939, pp.1 & 4

(9) Daily Notes, September 26, 1939, p. 1

(10) Daily Notes, September 27, 1939, pp. 1&3

(11) Daily Notes, September 28, 1939, p.4

(12) Daily Notes, October 2, 1939, pp. 1 & 2

(13) Daily Notes, October 3, 1939, pp. 1 & 2

(14) Daily Notes, October 16, 1939, p. 1 & 2

(15) Daily Notes, September 25, 1939, p.1

(16) Daily Notes, September 26, 1939, p. 1 & 3

(17) Daily Notes, November 10, 1939, p.1

(18) Daily Notes, November 16, 1939, p. 1

(19) Daily Notes, November 21, 1939, p. 1

(20) Daily Notes, February 13, 1940, p.1

(21) Daily Notes, May 2, 1940, pp. 1 & 7